COMMON GROUND

THE WATER, EARTH, AND AIR WE SHARE

MOLLY BANG

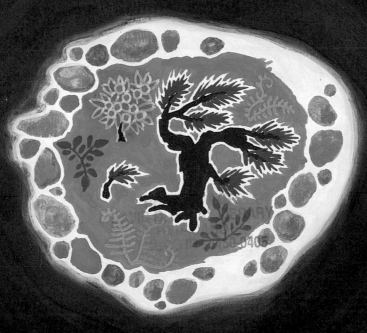

THE BLUE SKY PRESS
An Imprint of Scholastic Inc. · New York

THE BLUE SKY PRESS

For information regarding permission,

please write to: Permissions Department,

The Blue Sky Press, an imprint of Scholastic Inc.,

557 Broadway, New York, New York 10012.

The Blue Sky Press is a registered

trademark of Scholastic Inc.

Library of Congress catalog card number: 96-49618

The author wishes to thank biologist Garrett Hardin

for his inspiring article on population and the dilemma

of shared resources, "The Tragedy of the Commons,"

published in *Science*, volume 162, in 1968.

ISBN 0-590-10056-4

10 9 8 7 6

Printed in Singapore   46

First printing, October 1997

Production supervision by Angela Biola

Designed by Molly Bang and Kathleen Westray

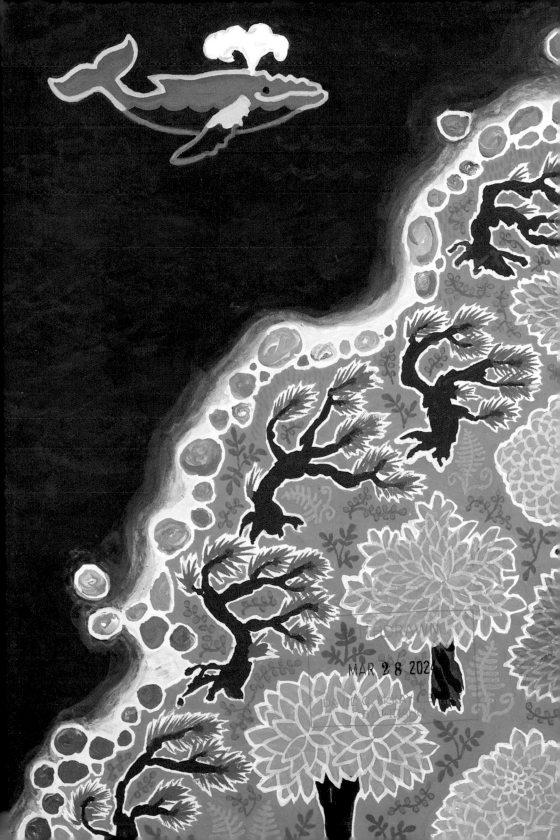

MAY WE MAKE OUR DECISIONS

FOR THE SEVENTH GENERATION.

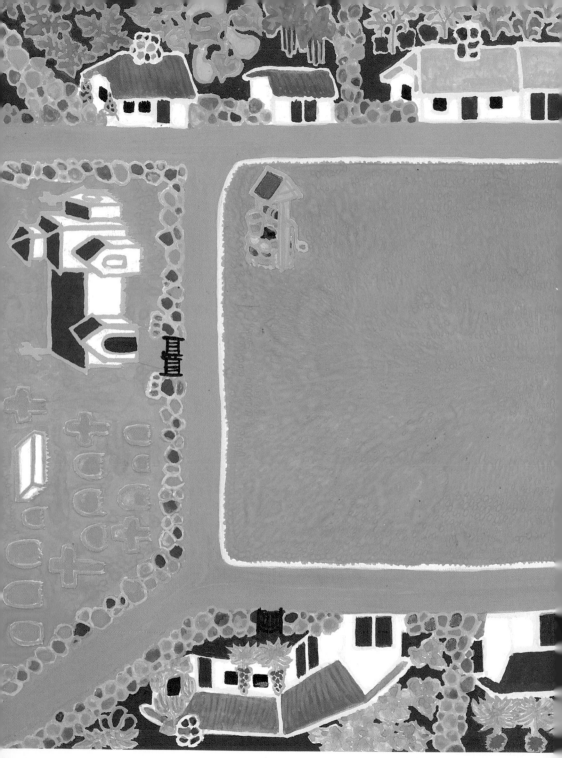

Long ago, a village was built around a commons.

The commons was "common ground"
which belonged to everyone in the village.

**All the villagers could bring their sheep
to the commons to graze.**

But there was a problem.

A villager who owned many sheep used more
of the commons than a villager who owned
a few sheep, or one, or none at all.

And because the common grass was free, people
put as many sheep to graze there as they could.
Soon there were too many sheep.

There was not enough grass for all of them.
This was not good for the commons, or for the sheep,
or for the villagers. So people did one of two things.

Some people stayed in the village, but
they made a plan together. They agreed
to keep the commons lush and green,
and to do a better job of sharing it.

Each person could only put one sheep
on the commons.
Everyone had to follow this rule.
Other people chose to move away.

There was always someplace else to go.

Today the world is much like that village.
Now our commons are our parks, reserves,

and natural resources, and the waters
and air of the whole world.
Today we have almost the same problem
that the villagers had.

Today each fisherman tries to catch as many fish as he can from the common sea.

This way, the fisherman has more fish to sell—
in the short run.

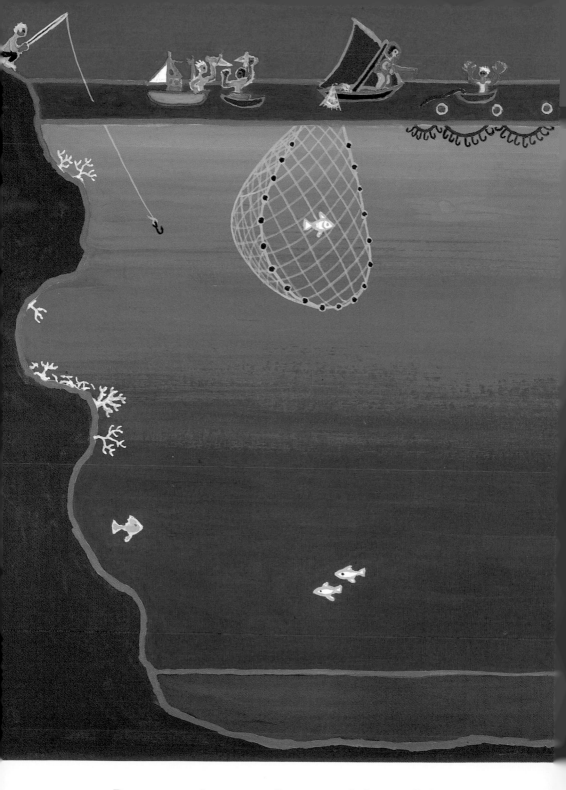

But soon there are fewer and fewer fish.

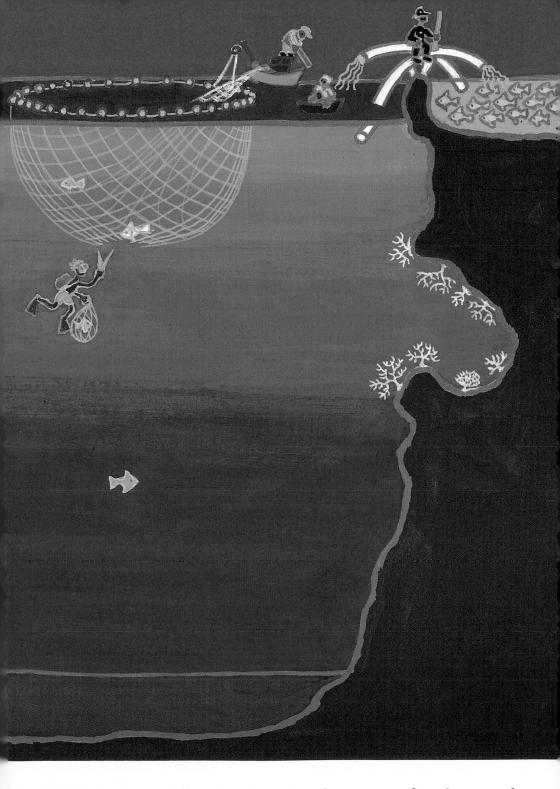

This is not good for the fish, for the sea, or for the people.

Today each lumber company wants to cut down as many trees as it can, to sell for wood, paper, and fuel.

The more trees the lumber company cuts down,
the more money it makes—in the short run.

But after cutting down so many trees,
there are fewer and fewer forests.

**This is not good for the trees,
or the forest creatures, or the forest soil.**

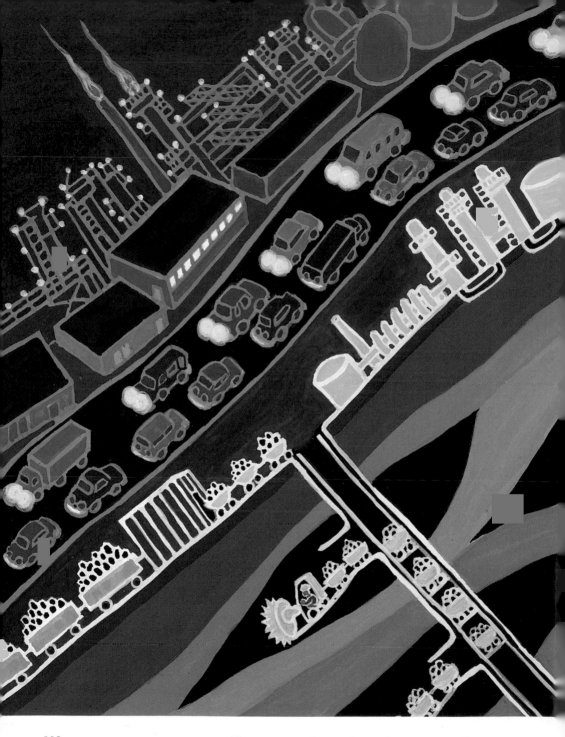

We use our common oil, gas, and coal to heat our houses and run our cars. Companies use them to make plastics and other chemicals.

In this way, we can stay warm, travel long distances, and visit stores full of amazing things to buy— in the short run.

But someday, these fossil fuels will be used up.

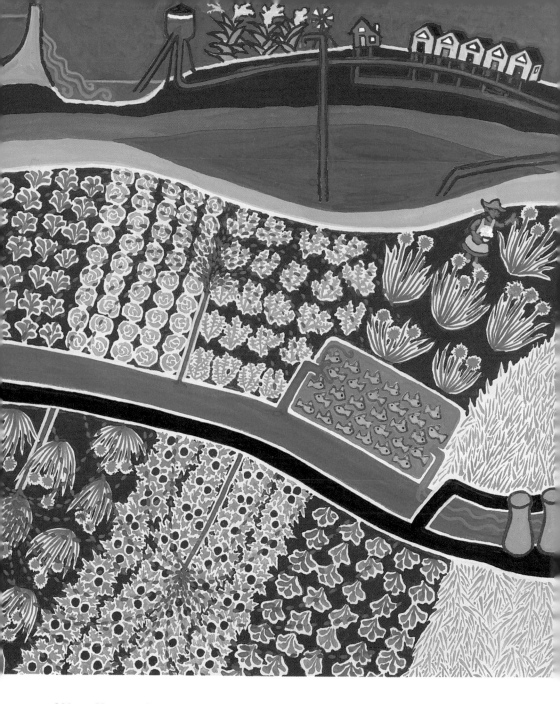

We all need water for drinking, cooking, and washing.
Farms need water for crops and livestock.
And businesses need water to cool equipment
and clean up wastes.

So we pump as much of our common water
as we can.
This works pretty well—
in the short run.

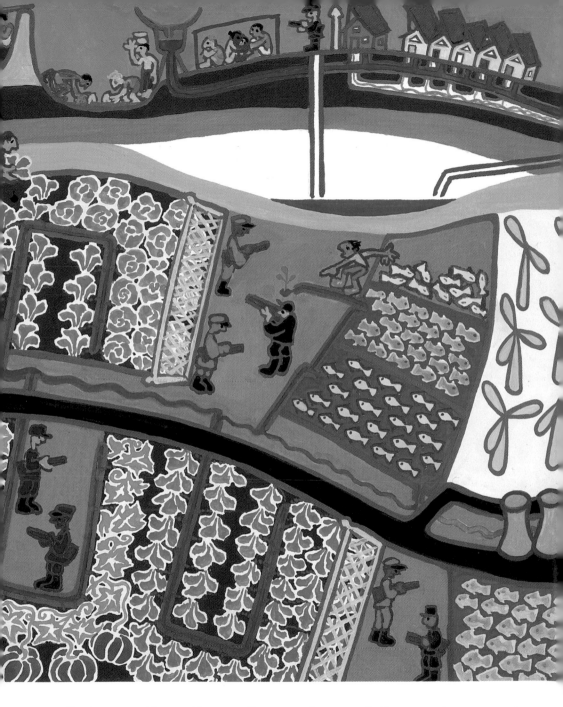

But over time, the wells run dry, and the wastes
pollute the water.
There is not enough clean water for all the people,
the farms, and the businesses.

Fresh water, fossil fuels, forests, fish—
one by one, we are destroying the natural
resources that sustain our lives.

So then, here is our common question:

If our country, our companies, and each

one of us benefit more in the short run

from using as many natural resources

as we can, then what will stop us

from destroying our whole world—

our common ground?

We need to answer this question TOGETHER,

because today we are different from those

long-ago villagers in one very important way...

Now we don't have anyplace else to go.